PANIC!

STATION

FLY 1 *What's all this science like, Mavis?*

FLY 2 *Well, it's easier to digest than that sandwich, Betty!*

BOXTREE LTD

The publishers would like to thank the following for permission to
reproduce photographs:

British Airways, page 19
BBC Hulton Picture Library, pages 7 and 21
Ron & Christine Foord, page 16
The Mansell Collection, pages 11, 38 and 41
Science Photo Library, pages 13 (Richard Folwell); 15 (Simon Fraser); 23
(Nasa); 25 (Nasa); 27 (Martin Dohrn); 29 (Dr R. Clark & M.R. Goff); 35
(David Parker); 37 (Dr T.E. Thompson)
UPI/Bettman Newsphotos, page 32

All photographs of the characters appearing on the programme are
reproduced with the kind permission of Television South plc.

The publishers would also like to gratefully thank David May, Head of
Physics at St. Paul's School, London, for his assistance.

Contents

The Measure of Things

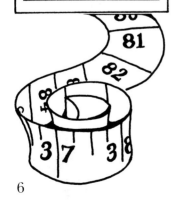

Oh, er, hello, Blister here – Minister for Science and Things. . . Sorry I'm so flustered – bit of a panic on at the moment – as usual! Well, the PM was on the hot-line just now. Call her the Prime Minister, she's more like the *Pry* Minister, wanting to know everything we get up to here at the department. This is supposed to be a *secret* department. I'm not even sure if I should know about it, and I'm the Minister. Oh dear. . .

Anyway, it seems the PM is rather concerned about how I'm measuring up in the job. Well, I asked Professor Shackleton and he said that measuring up is very important to scientists. I should have expected as much. To me things are either big or small or light or heavy, and if they're either big or heavy then I get Ferret to deal with them.

Scientists, however, need to know details much more precisely. They have to measure things accurately so that they can see whether they change and if so how, when they carry out their experiments.

What is matter?

Length, weight, volume and temperature are just some of the different aspects of what scientists call **matter.** Trees, buildings, chickens, bicycles, beefburgers, and everything else in the universe is made of matter – even the Prime Minister. Oh dear. . .

Matter has certain distinct properties: it takes up space and has what is known as **mass**, and it cannot be destroyed, only changed. This means that all the matter present in the universe today was present when the universe came into being about 15 thousand, million years ago.

Systems of measurement

Nowadays scientists all over the world use a standardised system for measuring physical qualities and quantities. Weights and lengths are stated using the Metric System. In the past, scientists in some countries used Imperial measurements such as ounces and pounds and feet and inches. This made it more difficult to understand each other's work so all scientists agreed to work in what are known as *SI UNITS*. (The letters *SI* stand for the French words 'Système International'.) The standard unit of mass is a kilogram, which is the mass of a solid cylinder of platinum-iridium alloy that is kept in an air-conditioned vault in Paris, under lock and key. All official metric masses in the world have been compared directly or indirectly to this.

Mass v. weight

Scientists refer to the *mass* of an object rather than its weight for a very simple reason. Answer this: Which is the heavier? An ant or an elephant? The answer seems obvious, but it isn't. On the surface of the Earth the elephant is many times heavier than the ant, but in outer space the elephant wouldn't weigh anything at all and would float around. The ant, back on Earth, would be heavier! This is because how much things weigh depends on gravity and there isn't any gravity acting on the elephant in space. Mass is a more scientific term because it considers how difficult it is to get something moving. You can move an ant with the flick of a finger, but an elephant takes a good deal more to shift. The mass of an object stays the same no matter where in the universe it may be.

To compare objects using scales you need to weigh them under the same conditions, where gravity acts on them equally. Kitchen scales are made only to show the correct weight of objects weighed on Earth. They wouldn't work on the moon, so that's one thing less to pack if you ever go there!

Substances also differ in their *density*. Density is a measure of how much matter there is in a certain volume of material. A household brick made from hardened clay is much heavier than a 'brick' the same size cut from expanded polystyrene. Hardened clay is said to be *denser* than polystyrene.

An Eggs-Periment With Density

If you take an ordinary uncooked hen's egg and place it in a glass of warm water it will sink. The egg is denser than the water. How can you get the egg to balance exactly midway between the top and bottom of the water? The answer is simple. Add table salt to the water and dissolve it by gentle stirring. (Don't break the egg!) Adding salt increases the amount of matter present in the water and it becomes more dense.

Eventually the density of the salty water is almost the same as that of the egg and the egg will hang in the middle of the glass.

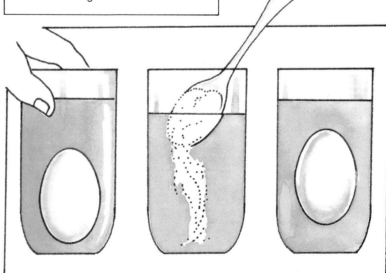

Water in the Dead Sea is so salty that it is dense enough to support even the laziest swimmer.

FLY 1 *Would Blister float in water?*

FLY 2 *I doubt it – I heard Lester say he was very dense!*

Little Things Mean a Lot

Now here's a seemingly simple, seriously scientific question. What's the smallest thing you can think of? A grain of rice? A speck of dust? Blister's brain? Well, whatever it is you've thought of, what would you end up with if you took that small thing and then cut it in half, then in half again, and again and again and again? – besides eyestrain and a blunt knife, that is!

The ancient Greek philosophers and scientists, people such as Aristotle and Plato, asked themselves the same question over 2500 years ago. Could you keep making something smaller forever, or was there a limit to how small a particle could be? They decided that you would reach a point where you could go no further and that all matter was made up from indivisible or unsplittable units which they called *atoms*. The word 'atom' means 'indivisible' in ancient Greek.

Modern ideas about atoms are based on the theories of an English chemist, John Dalton, published in 1808. Scientists have since shown that atoms actually exist. We know that they combine in various ways to form the different substances found in the universe.

Atoms and molecules

Atoms can be thought of as single building bricks from which matter is built up. There are many different types of these bricks, represented here by the different colours. Atoms may differ in size

and mass and in the properties they show – such as the way they react towards other atoms. Identical atoms, however, always behave alike.

The bricks can be put together to form larger structures which correspond to molecules. A molecule is the smallest portion of a substance that can exist on its own while still having all properties of the original substance. Some

How Small is Small?

Atoms really are tiny! And so are most of the molecules made from them. A teaspoonful of water contains over 150 thousand million, million, million water molecules. If the entire population of the world were to attempt to count them – working without sleep – it would take over 1 million years to do it!

substances can exist as single atoms, but a single atom of the gas oxygen isn't an oxygen molecule. Oxygen atoms pair up to form oxygen molecules – which is why oxygen (**O**) is always written as **O₂**.

If all the bricks in the structure are of the same type then it is known as an *element*. If the structure is a combination of different types of bricks then it is called a *compound*.

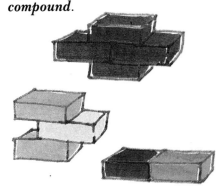

Compounds always have the same ratio of different atoms in them. Water, for example, is a compound of hydrogen and oxygen and always contains two atoms of hydrogen for every one atom of oxygen. In chemists' 'shorthand', a water molecule is written as **H₂O.**

Compounds are often quite different to the elements they are composed of. We have seen how water – a liquid – is formed from atoms of the two gases oxygen and hydrogen. Table salt – correctly called sodium chloride (**NaCl**) – is formed from sodium, a metal, and chlorine, a gas.

When compounds form, a *chemical reaction* is said to have taken place. However, not all different bricks will fit together to form a compound – some do not 'react'. Reactions can also occur between different molecules, where atoms are rearranged between them.

	Substance	Symbol	Nature
Metals	Aluminium	**Al**	A light metal.
	Copper	**Cu**	A reddish metal. A good conductor.
	Gold	**Au**	Soft heavy metal. Expensive.
	Iron	**Fe**	Very common metal. Steel is made from it.
	Mercury	**Hg**	An unusual liquid metal. Very shiny.
	Sodium	**Na**	A soft, very reactive metal.
	Tungsten	**W**	Metal used in light bulb filaments.
	Uranium	**U**	Heavy, radioactive metal.
Non-metals	Carbon	**C**	Found in several forms. Coal, diamond, etc.
	Sulphur	**S**	A yellow solid.
	Oxygen	**O**	A gas essential for life. Found in air.
	Nitrogen	**N**	Gas also found in air.
	Chlorine	**Cl**	Pungent yellowish-green gas. Used in bleach.
	Hydrogen	**H**	The simplest atom. A very light gas.

There are 92 different types of atoms found naturally in the universe – and therefore 92 different naturally-occurring elements. These range from hydrogen, the smallest atom, to uranium, the largest. They can be combined variously to form an almost unlimited number of molecules – which is why there are so many different substances in the universe. Elements are often denoted by symbols to save scientists from having to write out their names each time. The symbols of some common substances and their properties are shown in the table above.

Larger combinations of single molecules of a substance can be built up by repeating the same units. These often fit together in very specific ways, producing *crystals* in solids. The shapes of crystals reflect the shapes and arrangements of the molecules they contain.

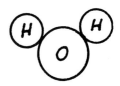

A water molecule (H₂0): 2 hydrogen atoms and 1 oxygen atom.

A nitrogen dioxide molecule (NO₂): 2 oxygen atoms and 1 nitrogen atom.

An hydrogen molecule (H₂).

An oxygen atom (O₂).

Atoms

Greetings fellow scholars – Prof. Rat PhD, MA, OBE here. (Old big 'ed!) Standby for an important piece of news: scientists get things wrong sometimes! Hard to believe, hey! Scientists occasionally get their facts wrong not because they're stupid (like Blister!) but because they don't know enough. This means that scientists sometimes have to guess about how things work. A scientific *theory* is really just an informed guess. That is why scientists need to carry out their experiments – they are looking for evidence to back up their ideas.

Now then, what's the point of me telling you all this? Well – despite what clever Dalton and the ancient Greeks thought, atoms are *not* the smallest bits of matter known to exist.

Dalton was right about a lot of things of course – he said that chemical reactions took place between atoms, for example. But he also said that atoms aren't divisible. The work of several scientists from the end of the nineteenth century onwards was to prove him wrong – notable amongst them a New Zealander, Ernest Rutherford, who became Lord Rutherford as a result.

What is an atom made of?

Atoms are made up of *fundamental particles*, of which there are three main types: *protons, neutrons* and *electrons.* They differ from each other in mass, in the electric charge they carry, and in their position in the atom. The protons and neutrons are found together in the *nucleus* in the centre of the atom, whilst the electrons whizz round it at high speed. The electrons are a little like planets orbiting the sun and they spin round in their orbits at the same time. Even the closest electrons are a comparatively massive distance away from the nucleus. If the full-stop at the end of this sentence is taken to be the nucleus of an atom, the electrons would be in a cloud about 10-15 metres away.

Electrons are very important

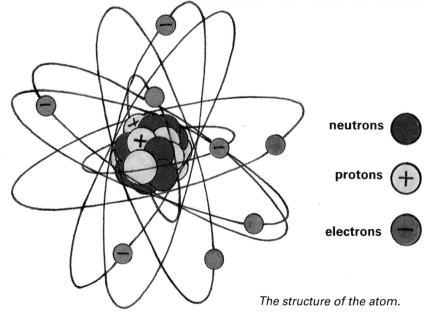

neutrons

protons

electrons

The structure of the atom.

because they are involved when different substances react – the electrons get moved from one atom to another or are shared between various atoms. The movement of electrons through a metal, such as a piece of wire, is what we call an *electric current*. Electricity! Not only does electricity power your television set but it is electrons fired out from a 'gun' at the back of the set that gives you a picture on the screen. Next time you get told off for watching too much TV just say that you're studying some electrons! That's seriously scientific!

There are always an equal number of protons and electrons in an atom. The electrons have a negative electrical charge (shown by the symbol −) which is balanced by the positive electrical charge on the protons (shown by the symbol +). An *electrostatic attraction* between the charges on the electrons and protons keeps the electrons in orbit around the nucleus and stops them flying off. Neutrons have no charge.

Electrons are very light in comparison to protons and neutrons, about 1/1840 of their mass. Protons and neutrons are roughly the same size and mass, and contribute most to the mass of a substance.

The simplest atom, hydrogen, consists of just a single electron orbiting around a single proton. The number of protons in the nucleus of an atom is very important as it is this characteristic that decides what element an atom belongs to. It is called the *atomic number* or *proton number*. Larger atoms have lots of protons. The number of neutrons in the nucleus of an atom can vary – even though the number of protons stays the same. This means that

The Greeks thought that atoms were the smallest bits of matter in the universe. Today, thanks to the work of scientists like Lord Ernest Rutherford above, we know that this is not so.

atoms of the same substance can have different masses. These are called *isotopes*.

Which is the biggest atom of them all?

Uranium nuclei are large and heavy because they contain over 140 neutrons and 92 protons. All these protons and neutrons packed together in a small space gives uranium an unstable nucleus and is responsible for uranium being radioactive. Very strong forces are required to keep all the protons and neutrons together in the nucleus. Even though uranium has the largest atoms found in nature, a single uranium atom still only weighs 0.000 000 000 000 000 000 0004 grams.

FLY 1 *Why are neutrons cheap?*

FLY 2 *Because there's no charge!*

11

What State Are You In?

Hi! Some things in the laboratory here at the station are **solid**, other things are a **gas**. Substances may be made up from the same molecules yet exist in completely different forms – like water, H_2O, for example. Water can be found as ice, or ordinary drinking water, or the steam from a boiling kettle, but it still consists of the same H_2O molecules in each case.

The states of matter

Ice, water, and steam are the **solid**, **liquid**, and **gaseous states** of water. A '**state**' is the physical condition of a substance. Everything in the world is in one of these three states – solid, liquid or gas.

The explanation for the different states lies in the structure or arrangement of the molecules.

IN SOLIDS molecules are arranged in regular patterns with more or less fixed positions. They are **bonded** to their neighbouring molecules with only small spaces between them. This is why solids are rigid. The molecules move a little, but because they are fixed they can only vibrate, which they do about one point. These vibrations are very, very fast – over 50 million, million times a second. It is the vibration of the molecules in a quartz crystal that allows digital watches to keep such precise time.

When solids are stretched their molecules are pulled further apart, which is what happens when you stretch a steel spring. The steel spring goes back to its original shape when you stop pulling on it because the molecules return to their original positions. This is a phenomenon called **elasticity**.

IN LIQUIDS the molecules move about more, changing neighbours all the time but staying at a more or less constant distance apart. This means that liquids can be poured but not easily compressed. They will still occupy the same amount of space.

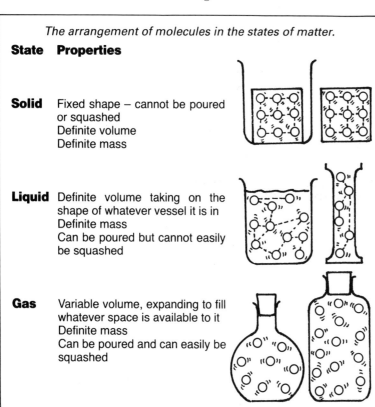

The arrangement of molecules in the states of matter.

State	Properties
Solid	Fixed shape – cannot be poured or squashed Definite volume Definite mass
Liquid	Definite volume taking on the shape of whatever vessel it is in Definite mass Can be poured but cannot easily be squashed
Gas	Variable volume, expanding to fill whatever space is available to it Definite mass Can be poured and can easily be squashed

IN GASES the molecules are practically independent of each other and move about at high speeds in all directions. Hydrogen is the fastest moving gas and the molecules travel at about two kilometres per second, or over 3000 miles per hour at room temperature! They don't normally travel in straight lines as they keep bumping into each other.

See For Yourself!

Place an opened bottle of perfume a few metres away from you in a room. Eventually molecules of scent reach your nose and you are able to smell the perfume. This movement of scent molecules through the air is called *diffusion*. Provided there is no strong draught in the room you should be able to smell the perfume in the air on all sides of the bottle, showing that molecules move randomly in all directions. The scent molecules keep colliding with those in the air and bouncing off in new directions, like moving snooker balls hitting each other.

Diffusion takes place in liquids also. If you add a few drops of food-colouring or ink to a beaker of still water, eventually the whole volume of water will take on the colour of the dye.

So what happens when solid ice forms liquid water? Good question. Heating ice gives the molecules more energy so that they start to move about more, away from their fixed positions, and begin to slide over each other. This is called *melting*. Most solids will melt provided they are heated up enough.

To turn water into steam – a liquid into gas – you need to give the molecules even more energy so that they move apart and become independent of each other. This is what happens when you heat water so that it *boils*. Some liquids will boil at quite low temperatures. Your skin feels cold when you put deodorant or perfume on it because they both contain liquid alcohol which *evaporates* into a gas taking away a little heat from your body. You have acted as a human kettle! Some substances are unusual in that they will turn from a solid into a gas without becoming a liquid first. This is called *sublimation*. You've probably seen this happen with the 'dry ice' used to create atmosphere at pop concerts. 'Dry ice' is actually solid, frozen carbon dioxide which vaporises immediately at room temperature.

Of course, you can turn a gas back into a liquid or a liquid into a solid by cooling it down. This takes away energy from the molecules. Turning liquid water into ice is called *freezing*. Water vapour in the air turns back into liquid water when it loses heat, often by coming into contact with a cold surface such as a window. This is called *condensation* and is the reason for the pools of water you find on your window sills on cold winter mornings.

This gas jar contains vaporising 'dry ice': the white fumes are water droplets forming in the air.

Water, Water, Everywhere

Hello there! What's incredibly common and really rather amazing at the same time? No, it isn't Lester . . . it's water. Did you know that 70 per cent of the Earth's surface is covered with water? (A little more than that when the Professor forgets to turn the bathwater off!) Water is vital to the maintenance of life on Earth – the human race and all animals and plants are completely dependent on it – and astronomers consider its presence on other planets in the universe a good sign that they might also support life. So, don't complain next time it rains!

The water cycle

Rain is an important part of the *water cycle*. This is the name given to the process by which all the water on our planet continually moves between the land, the sea, and the sky – and has done for millions of years. Heat from the sun causes water to evaporate from open surfaces such as oceans, lakes, and rivers, and to rise into the air. This water vapour is then carried high into the atmosphere by air currents, where it cools and condenses to form clouds of ice particles higher up, or water droplets lower down. When these droplets grow too heavy they fall back down as rain, hail or snow, depending on the temperature. This is called *precipitation*. A lot of the water runs back into the sea via rivers and streams, and the whole process then starts all over again.

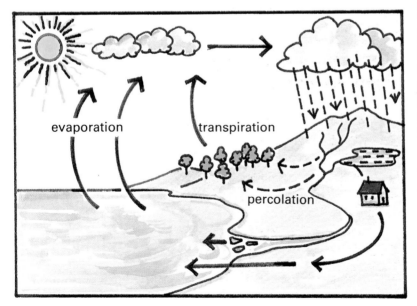

Water and solubility

Water is a good *solvent* – this means that many different substances will dissolve in it, including sugar, salt, rocks, metals and gases just to mention a few. (Substances that will dissolve in liquids are known as *solutes*.)

Did you know that fish are able to breathe in water because of the oxygen dissolved in it? Or that when you drink a glass of water you also swallow a few molecules of the glass. This is a very tiny amount though, which is why your crockery doesn't need replacing every week.

One hundred per cent pure water is very rare in nature, if it exists at all. Scientists can make it in laboratories, where it is called *distilled water*.

Icebergs can be a danger to vessels because they float about and may turn up unexpectedly. If ice was denser than water it would sink to the ocean floor and stay put – where it would be less of a hazard.

When it rains, many gases in the air dissolve into the rain – including carbon dioxide (CO_2) and sulphur dioxide (SO_2). In areas of high pollution, this can result in a problem known as *acid rain*. Here the rainfall contains many dissolved substances that are harmful to plants, animals and buildings. It will even eat away stone. Acid rain is a major environmental hazard and can be controlled by restricting the amount of smoke released from factory chimneys.

Carbon dioxide in water can have less dangerous consequences, however. CO_2 is dissolved into water at high pressure to make fizzy drinks. The 'tart' taste these drinks have is because they are slightly acidic.

What happens to water when it freezes

Water being so common, we take many of its rather odd properties for granted. For example, did it ever strike you as being unusual that ice should float in water? You would normally expect the solid phase of a substance to be denser and heavier than the liquid, but water actually expands and becomes lighter when it freezes. This is why ice floats. Water is at its maximum density at 4°C, a little above its freezing point of 0°C.

The water molecule

For such an amazing liquid, water really is a very simple molecule made up of two hydrogen atoms and one of oxygen, or H_2O as it is written.

Model of a water molecule.

O = Oxygen atom
H = Hydrogen atom

Molecules of water are formed every time an *organic* material such as wood or paper is burnt in air. Strange to think that burning involves the production of water when the Fire Brigade use water to put out fires!

Molecules of H_2O have a strong attraction for their fellow liquid water molecules. Have you noticed how water seems to have a 'skin' on it? You can see this clearly by gently over-filling a glass with water – a curved surface is formed when the water level rises above the level of the glass. This phenomenon – which is also found in other liquids – is called *surface tension*. The molecules at the surface of a volume of water effectively join up with and support each other. They are pulled inwards by the other molecules inside the water. Surface tension will even support the weight of a steel needle. See for yourself! Float a piece of tissue paper on the surface of some water. Then gently lay a sewing needle on top of it. The tissue paper will eventually absorb water and sink, leaving the needle supported on the water by surface tension.

Surface tension allows insects such as pondskaters to walk across the surface of ponds without falling in. Their long legs help spread their weight and reduce the risk.

While water molecules are attracted to each other they are also attracted to the molecules of other substances, sometimes more so. This is why raindrops stick or *adhere* to windows. (Attraction between molecules of the same substance is called *cohesion*, between different molecules it is called *adhesion*.

FLY 1 *Ugh! I think soap and water was a terrible invention.*

FLY 2 *Yes – that idea wouldn't 'wash' with me!*

Because water molecules are more attracted to glass molecules than to each other water rises up inside thin glass tubes placed in it. The thinner the tube the higher it goes. This is called *capillarity*. Water molecules at the edges are attracted to the glass molecules and rise up, pulling their neighbouring molecules with them. This doesn't just occur with glass and water. If you were to dip a sugar cube partway into a cup of coffee, the coffee would rise up into the cube through tiny passages between the sugar crystals. Blotting paper absorbs water because it consists of lots of fine pores. Capillarity is also partly responsible for the movement of water up the stems of plants. You could say the water 'travels by tube'!

The attraction between oil and water molecules is less than that between just water molecules – which is why oil and water don't mix. They form what is known as an *emulsion*. The molecules separate out eventually, which is why you get two layers in bottles of salad dressing, with the oil on top because it is the less dense liquid of the two.

Adding a *detergent* to water allows it to wash away oil because the molecules of detergent are attracted to both the water and oil molecules and link them up. This is why we use soap to wash with.

How To Turn White Carnations Red

The stems of plants contain fine tubes through which their water supply moves and which act as fine capillaries. Place the cut stem of a white carnation into some water to which red ink has been added. Several hours later the petals of the flower will be streaked with red. The coloured water has passed up the stem and into the fine passageways in the petals.

What an Atmosphere!

The Minister came rushing into the laboratory the other day, panicking as usual, and saying that he was under a lot of pressure. Well, I said, of course you are – we all are. We all have something pressing against us all the time – it's the air. The reason you don't notice it is that it presses against you all over in all directions equally, which is why you don't bend or fall over. We say that the air exerts *atmospheric pressure.*

You'd never get a decent cup of tea on Mount Everest – just when you think you might need one most! Because of the low air pressure at high altitudes, water boils at a much lower temperature, and if you've ever tried to make tea with lukewarm water. . . yeuch!

What is air pressure?

Air pressure exists because air is heavy, it has weight. The atmosphere around our planet extends upwards over 400 kilometres above sea-level and changes in constitution with increasing *altitude*. (Altitude is a more technical word for height.) The atmosphere is thought of as being in several different layers (see diagram below), but generally speaking there is less and less air the higher up you go. The air is said to get 'thinner', or less dense.

The atmosphere is held around the Earth by gravity, which is why there is a greater density of air at lower altitudes – and consequently, a greater air pressure. Air at sea-level exerts a pressure of

The earth's atmosphere is 600km thick and can be divided into four regions, from the troposphere, the lowest layer, to the exosphere, the highest region which merges into empty space.

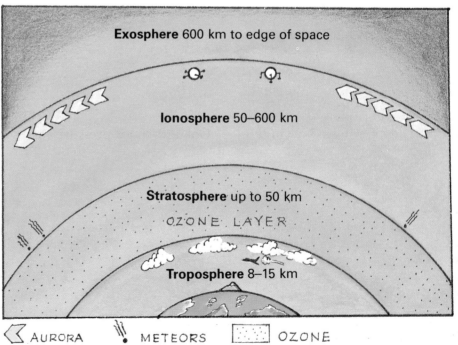

Exosphere 600 km to edge of space

Ionosphere 50–600 km

Stratosphere up to 50 km

OZONE LAYER

Troposphere 8–15 km

AURORA METEORS OZONE

18

about 100,000 newtons per square metre, but it is impossible to give a set figure for air pressure because it varies all over the globe – due to both altitude and temperature. A pressure of 100,000 newtons per square metre is almost exactly the same as the effect of having the weight of a kilogram block sitting on every square centimetre of the surface of an object. To help you picture this more easily, this would be like living with a kilo bag of sugar pressing on every square centimetre of your skin. Quite a load!

Most people in the world are used to living with air pressure roughly the same as that at sea-level – 100,000 newtons per square metre. For this reason the cabins of high-flying aircraft have to be *pressurised* – they have their own sealed-in atmosphere. Without this, passengers would feel very uncomfortable as the air pressure at high altitude is very low.

See For Yourself!

Prove to yourself that air pressure exists. Place a ruler partway over the edge of a table and lay a sheet of newspaper on top, smoothing it down gently. Now, strike the exposed end of the ruler. You should find that the ruler is held in place against the table by air pressing down on the newspaper. The force is really quite strong – you could break the ruler if you're not careful.

As air pressure at high altitudes is very low, the cabins of high-flying aircraft have to be pressurised.

Changes in air pressure correspond with changes in the weather. Colder air is denser and exerts a higher pressure than warm air. Areas of high and low pressure are often shown on weather maps.

Air pressure also changes when air moves – a fact first investigated by the Swiss scientist Bernoulli. Flowing air exerts a lower pressure than stationary air. To prove this for yourself, try the two experiments in the box at the bottom of page 20.

What a gas!

All right then, so what is air? You can't taste it, you can't smell it, and you can't see it – but you can see it pushing things about – and air does have mass, it is heavy. Air is in fact a mixture of gases (see table on opposite page). It is, however, not a **compound**. This means that all the gases in the air can be separated from each other without the use of chemical processes, and you could easily make your own air by adding together the correct amounts of each of the components.

CARBON DIOXIDE The air we breathe out of our bodies has a slightly higher proportion of carbon dioxide in it and slightly less oxygen than is found in atmospheric air. Some of the oxygen is absorbed in our lungs, and the carbon dioxide is a waste product of the processes that turn the food we eat into energy for our muscles. Carbon dioxide stays at such a low percentage in the air because it is taken in by plants which produce oxygen in return.

Carbon dioxide is a heavy gas produced every time when an organic substance such as wood or paper is burnt in air. It will not support burning itself and is used in fire extinguishers, where it is mixed with foam.

Make Your Own Fire Extinguisher

Carbon dioxide gas is generated when you add a mild acid such as vinegar or lemon juice to bicarbonate of soda. Put several teaspoonfuls of bicarbonate of soda in the bottom of a jam-jar and add vinegar or lemon juice so that it fizzes quite strongly. (There is no need to cover the jar because CO_2 is heavier than air.) Now ask your mum or dad to help you with the next bit. Introduce a lighted taper into the jar, and see what happens.

INERT GASES Though most of the air is made up of nitrogen, it is a rather boring gas that doesn't do much. The other gases in the air do even less and are called *inert gases* for that very reason. That doesn't mean that they don't have

their uses. Argon and neon, for example, are used in electric lights.

HYDROGEN is the lightest gas and it is also possibly the most explosive when mixed with air. Because it is so light hydrogen was used for buoyancy in airships until the Hindenburg disaster.

*The Hindenburg was the largest, most luxurious airship the world had ever seen – over twice the length of a football pitch, and filled with potentially explosive hydrogen gas. Ironically, she was on her final flight in May 1937 when disaster struck. Coming in to land at New York, she exploded. Few people were killed, however, because the hydrogen flame radiated very little heat and the passengers were carried beneath the balloon, where it was cooler. Today airships are filled with **helium**, which is very expensive but does not burn.*

The Composition of Air	
Gas	**Percentage in air**
Nitrogen	78%
Oxygen	21%
Argon	0.9%
Water vapour (variable)	
Carbon Dioxide	
Neon	0.1%
Helium	
Krypton	
Xenon	
Hydrogen (a trace)	

Hello Suckers!

Hello there. Now for some really serious science! Gases are a little like flies – they're not too keen on being squashed! Put your finger over the end of a bicycle pump and try pushing the handle down all the way. Not easy is it? And it's all due to molecules again!

You can feel the resistance of air to being squashed when you pump up a bicycle tyre. It gets harder to push more air through the valve. The air inside the tyre is **compressed**, and is said to be at a high pressure.

Air rushes out of a tyre when you have a puncture because of the difference in pressure to the air outside. Balloons – and sometimes tyres! – explode when you puncture them because all the pressurised air inside tries to rush out through a rather small hole at once, rupturing the surrounding material.

How To Stick A Pin In A Balloon Without It Exploding

This is a clever trick. Inflate a balloon and challenge a friend to stick a pin into it without it exploding. It can be done! When they give up, stick a square of adhesive tape onto the balloon and put the pin through this. The tape holds the skin of the balloon together and stops it from going BANG!

Gases and liquids at different pressures want to **equilibriate**, this means that they want to become the same pressure all over, and they always flow from areas of high pressure to those of lower pressure. (Pressure is measured in newtons per square metre (N/m^2).) Gases at very high pressures can become liquids if they are

See For Yourself!

Wrap plasticine round a drinking straw and wedge it firmly into the neck of a partly-filled bottle of water. The seal must be air-tight. Now blow hard down the straw into the bottle so that bubbles of air pass through the water. Take the straw away from your mouth and water will shoot out of it like a fountain. The air inside the bottle expands when the pressure due to blowing is removed. This forces the water back out of the straw.

Space-walking astronauts must wear pressurised suits to prevent their blood from boiling away into the vacuum around them.

cooled, and become gases again when the pressure is removed.

Air pressure in a vacuum

The lowest pressures that exist are found in *vacuums.* A perfect vacuum is a space with absolutely nothing in it whatsoever, a little bit like Blister's skull! Space is often thought of as a perfect vacuum but it contains all sorts of rubbish, planets, dust, spaceships and so on, though there are possibly areas far off in deep space with nothing whatsoever in them.

The term 'vacuum' is generally used to describe any space containing a pressure lower than atmospheric air pressure.

Liquids will boil at lowered temperatures in vacuums because there are so few air molecules pushing down on them, stopping bubbles of vapour forming in the liquid. Conversely, liquids boil at higher temperatures at higher pressures because they have *more* molecules pressing down on them. Pressure-cookers work in this way.

Down to Earth

The Minister made one of his far too frequent visits to the laboratory recently, just as I was settling down to another day flat out – with my feet up in my favourite armchair, that is! 'Oh dear,' he gibbered, 'I've got this really difficult question to answer. Listen, if you drop a cannonball and a tennis ball from the same height, which hits the ground first?'

What do you think the answer is? You're probably wrong. . . Try the experiment yourself, but if you don't have a cannonball handy, any two things obviously different in weight will do – a tennis ball and a tight ball of paper for example. (Nothing breakable please!)

Regardless of weight, the two things will hit the ground at the same time. All things fall to the ground with the same *acceleration* because they are all subject to the same force: *gravity*. (All right, I know a flat sheet of paper takes longer to fall than a crumpled ball of paper, and that a parachutist will fall slower than a skydiver – but that's because the air gets in the way. In a vacuum they'd all hit the ground together, and very fast. Ouch!)

Gravitational force

For centuries people believed that heavy objects fell faster than light ones – who were they to disagree with the Greek philosopher Aristotle. The Italian scientist Galileo Galilei didn't agree, and he began dropping things from the top of the Leaning Tower of Pisa to prove his point. The great English scientist Sir Isaac Newton (1642-1727) started thinking about

gravity after an apple fell on his head, or at least that's how the story goes! Newton didn't invent or discover gravity – it has always existed and people had noticed it before – but he was the first to work out important laws about it.

Gravity exists because matter is attracted to all other matter and exerts a 'pull' on it called a ***gravitational force***. The more massive an object is (the more matter there is present) then the greater its gravitational attraction is. So, to go back to Newton and his apple, not only is the apple attracted to the Earth – which is why it falls down – but the Earth is also attracted to the apple. You don't see the Earth move up because the planet is so huge and its movement is unnoticeable. *You* exert a gravitational pull on everything else around you but because you're not at all massive compared to the Earth things don't move through the air to stick to you.

The gravitational attraction between objects decreases the further apart they are, but planets and stars are so huge that they exert gravitational influences over great distances across space. The giant gravitational pull of the sun, about 150 million kilometres away from Earth, keeps all the planets

The gravitational pull of the Earth is very strong: rockets need to be very powerful to escape it and travel out into space.

Centre of gravity

But let's come back down to Earth with a bump. Gravity acts on all parts of an object, but is thought of as only acting on just one point, and this is known as the *centre of gravity*. Things fall over when this centre of gravity isn't supported. The centre of gravity of a 30 cm ruler is exactly half-way along its length and across its width. A ruler will balance on your finger tip at this point. Anywhere else and the ruler falls off.

Tall objects are more likely to fall over than squat objects because their centre of gravity becomes unsupported sooner when they are made to lean over. Putting more weight at the bottom of a tall object brings its centre of gravity closer to the ground and makes it harder to tip over. For the same reasons, racing cars are very low slung so that they are less likely to roll over at bends.

FLY 1 *Why does Blister take this subject so seriously?*

FLY 2 *He must realise the gravity of the situation!*

The centre of gravity of an object affects its stability. If you push an object a little it will fall back to its original position (A). But if you push it too far, its centre of gravity becomes unsupported and it will fall over (B).

in the solar system in orbit around itself, and the gravitational pull of the moon attracts water on the surface of Earth and is responsible for the daily tides.

Astro-physicists have proposed the existence of so-called 'black holes' – super-dense regions of space, packed with matter – that exert gigantic gravitational forces, pulling yet more matter into them. Nothing can escape! This makes them even more massive, so that they attract even more matter, and so on. The nearest black hole to Earth is thought to be about 6500 light years away – which is why we haven't all been sucked into it. Try not to worry about it!

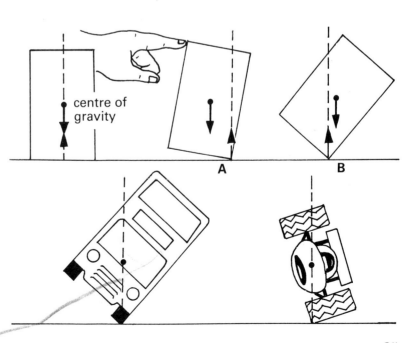

centre of gravity

A   B

Very Energetic!

Playing the drums in a swinging jazz combo every night, like I do, some days I just don't feel I have the *energy* to do any *work*. These days are known as 'weekdays' – when I don't really do anything other than catch up on my sleep. (Weekends I spend relaxing – it doesn't pay to overdo it!)

Scientists define **energy** as the potential to do work, which simply means that without energy machines will not run. There are lots of different sources of energy in the universe. Energy is measured in joules (J).

Sources of energy

A moving object possesses what is called **kinetic energy**. This is obvious in a large moving object like a cricket ball or a car but can also be considered on a molecular scale. The kinetic energy possessed by the particles of a substance affect its state. Gas molecules have more kinetic energy than those of a solid or liquid phase.

Kinetic energy can be harnessed and used to drive machines: windmills run on kinetic energy taken from the air, and the kinetic energy of flowing water will turn waterwheels and drive turbines.

Of course, things don't have to move to possess energy. Torch batteries, food and radioactive substances, for example, all store energy and they are stationary. They contain stored or **potential energy** which can be transferred so that it is capable of driving a machine or doing work. The energy obtained from a battery is stored in the chemicals inside. It

If all the matter in a 30 kg child could be converted into energy it would be enough to run a one-bar electric fire for 85 million years! That's a thought to keep you warm in winter!

contains substances that react together to produce electricity. (When this reaction has stopped we say the battery is 'flat'.) The battery's energy can be transferred to kinetic energy by connecting the battery to a motor.

Raising an object above the ground gives it **gravitational potential energy**. It is this which is used to run a grandfather clock. The energy is stored in heavy metal weights that are raised up in the process of winding up the clock. The weights then slowly descend inside the case and energy is transferred to turn the hands.

The food we eat contains energy that is transferred by digestion. Part ends up in our muscles and this allows us to move. We also get hotter at the same time – which is why athletes are said to be 'warming up' when they jog about before competing. This illustrates an important point: energy can be transferred from one place to another with varying degrees of ease.

Energy from the sun

Most of the energy on Earth comes directly or indirectly from the sun via heat or light. Plants transfer some of this energy by a process called *photosynthesis* into 'chemical' energy in stored carbohydrates. Animals obtain energy by munching on the plants and may themselves be munched on by other animals. The planet's fossil fuel reserves – oil, coal, and gas – are formed from the remains of organisms that lived on Earth thousands of years ago.

Energy from the sun also drives the winds and lifts up water from the oceans, giving it potential energy.

The only comparable amount of energy to come from anything other than the sun is the energy released in a nuclear explosion, yet it is nowhere near as powerful.

The sun's energy comes from a process called *nuclear fusion* that takes place deep at the heart of the star. It will eventually stop, but not for millions of years, so it shouldn't affect your summer holidays!

Energy loss

Energy is always *conserved* – which means that it can never be created or destroyed, only transferred from body to body. Energy seems to disappear because it often ends up as 'heat' or *thermal energy* which is hard to store and difficult to tranfer back to its origins.

Machines are never 100 per cent efficient in converting one form of energy into another because of *friction*. Friction is the external force that acts to change the speed of movement of objects. It results from the attraction between molecules at the surface of an object and the surface of the material it is in contact with. Friction between surfaces tends to 'generate' heat as surface molecules gain energy and start to vibrate more. This is why our hands feel warmer when we rub them together. In fact energy is not generated at all; it is simply transferred from energy stored in fuel inside out bodies via the process of rubbing our hands together. In the same way machines 'lose' some energy as heat.

Ancient peoples worshipped the sun as a god. An eclipse of the sun threw them into a panic – they did not know that it was just the moon casting a shadow on the Earth and that it would only last a few minutes. The photograph below shows a partial eclipse of the sun.

The changing energy of a windfall apple.

POTENTIAL ENERGY

KINETIC ENERGY

HEAT ENERGY

The Heat is On!

Hi there! Lester may think he plays hot music and acts cool but I bet he doesn't know what heat actually is – and saying that is bound to make his temperature rise!

Thermal energy

Heat (or thermal energy) is the energy molecules possess because of their vibration. As this involves movement, thermal energy is partly just a special form of kinetic energy. The hotter a substance is the more its molecules vibrate and if these vibrations become great enough then a solid may melt to become a liquid and a liquid evaporate to become a vapour.

The molecules in a material vibrate more as it becomes hotter taking up more space. The material *expands* as a result and its volume increases. On cooling, the molecules come closer together again and the material *contracts*.

The liquid in a thermometer expands when exposed to heat and is pushed along inside the tube. The tube is calibrated to show the temperature associated with the degree of expansion.

We often talk about the *temperature* of an object but temperature is not a direct measurement of the thermal energy it contains. A thimbleful of boiling water will register a higher temperature on a thermometer than a swimming pool full of warm water, but the water in the pool contains more thermal energy because there are so many more molecules in it, even though their individual energies are less. To use a thermometer to compare thermal energies you need to consider similar numbers of molecules.

Measuring temperature

We use thermometers because we are bad at estimating temperatures: people just don't agree on what is hot and cold. Humans tend to relate all temperatures to their own body temperature – 37°C or thereabouts. Temperature receptors in our skin tell us when our environment or the things we touch are hotter or colder than this. They can be fooled quite easily. Go outside in winter and let your hands get really cold. If you then come indoors and place them under a cold tap the water will feel warm! This is because our receptors only *compare* temperatures: if our hands are colder than the water then we register it as being warm.

Scientists often use the Celsius scale for measuring temperatures, but another unit called a *kelvin* is used in serious thermodynamic studies. (*Thermodynamics* is the branch of science concerned with the effects of heat on matter.) The kelvin scale is named after the British scientist William Kelvin (1824-1907). One kelvin (1K) is exactly equal to one degree Celsius (1°C). Whereas the Celsius scale begins at the freezing point of water, zero kelvins (0K) or *absolute zero* is the coldest anything can ever be – it is the temperature at which molecules become perfectly still and have no vibrational energy whatsoever. It corresponds to a temperature of

FLY 1 *Why did Blister go jogging with a thermometer?*

FLY 2 *Well, I heard he was running a temperature!*

−273.15°C and has never yet been reached in laboratories. Above absolute zero all molecules have vibrational energy. This means that even cold things are hot – including cold school dinners!

Transferring heat energy

There are three ways energy can be transferred by heating:

CONDUCTION You've probably noticed that if you heat one end of a metal rod, heat passes down the length of the rod so that the far end becomes hot as well. This is called *conduction* of heat and some substances are better at it than others. Metals are very good *conductors*. Substances that do not conduct heat well are called *insulators*. Polystyrene, wool, water, cotton, air and straw are all good insulators. A vacuum is the best insulation of all though, because it contains no molecules to which thermal energy can be transferred. This is one of the ways in which a vacuum flask helps to keep things at a constant temperature. Hot objects usually cool down because energy is given away to air molecules that come into contact with them.

CONVECTION When substances get hot they expand and because of this their density is lowered: they become lighter. In gases and liquids the less dense material tends to rise above its cooler and denser surrounding material warming the cooler gas or liquid on the way. This method of heating is called *convection*. (It doesn't happen in solids because the molecules aren't free to move, only to vibrate.) *Convection currents* are often formed, particularly in air and water. Both hot

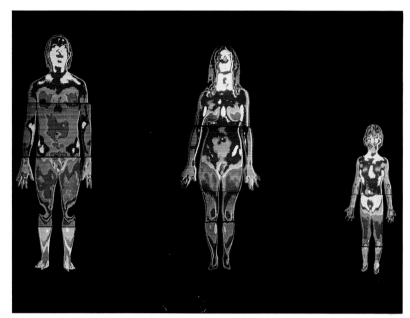

There are special cameras, sensitive to infra-red radiation, that will give colour-coded pictures of objects according to how hot they are. The temperature of the skin of a boy, woman and man is shown on the thermograph above, ranging from white for the hottest parts, through red, orange, green and blue for the coolest parts.

air and hot water rise away from the source of heat and cooler air or water flows in to take its place. Rising currents of hot air are called *thermals* and birds often use them to soar high in the air without having to flap their wings.

RADIATION A hot object like an electric fire will still feel warm from a distance even though we are not directly above it in the flow of warm air it generates. This is because it emits energy via *radiant heat*. This is most commonly what we call *infra-red radiation*. All hot objects emit a certain amount of radiant energy and it is the only way in which heat can be transferred through a vacuum. That is why the sun warms us even though it is millions of miles away in space.

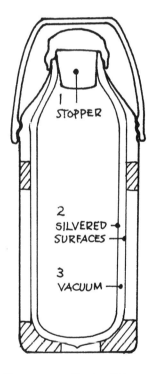

The vacuum flask will keep hot liquids hot or cold liquids cold. The features labelled below prevent heat transferrence by:
(1) convection;
(2) radiation;
(3) conduction.

29

Good Vibrations

Hi! I'm sure you'd agree (though I'm not so certain Lavinia would) that on saxophone I have a great *sound*. That much is obvious, but it isn't so clear what sound actually is. The Professor said it was a way of carrying energy but how is it we hear different notes and different volumes, and how does sound reach our ears?

What is sound?

Sound travels in the form of waves. **Sound waves** are made when a material moves backwards and forwards repeatedly against the substance which surrounds it. These repeated movements backwards and forwards are known as *vibrations*.

When a drum is hit with a stick, the skin of the drum begins to vibrate. As the skin vibrates, it stretches and squashes the layer of air around it, which in turn stretches and squashes the next layer of air, and so on. As the sound waves travel outwards they make the molecules in the air vibrate. This means that layers of air are continually moving backwards and forwards – being squashed and pulled – with the same frequency as the vibrating drum, and passing energy through the air. The energy of sound is transmitted in *longitudinal waves*.

Finally, the sound reaches the air pressing against the ear drum and vibrates. This is converted into nervous impulses that are interpreted in the brain as sound, which you can hear.

Sound waves do not only travel through the air. Sound will travel through all the states of matter – gas, solids and liquids, but it cannot travel through a vacuum. Sound has to have a medium through which to travel.

Hear For Yourself!

Take a 30 cm ruler. Hold the ruler down over the edge of the table and press down with your finger on the exposed end to make it 'twang'. You can see the end of the ruler vibrating. Though too fast to count with the eye, the number of times the end of the ruler vibrates up and down in a set period of time is important. The rate of vibration is known as the **frequency** and affects the pitch of the sound. The vibrating end of the ruler agitates the air in contact with it and makes it move back and forth with the same frequency. It gives the air energy which is transmitted through the air to your ears. If you shorten the exposed length of the ruler and 'twang' it again, the end of the ruler will vibrate faster and the pitch of the noise will be higher.

Remember, sound waves travel through all states of matter. As well as being able to hear the noise of the ruler through the air, you will also be able to hear it if you put your ear down against the table. Try it!

The experiment with the ruler has shown that the sound waves reaching our ears can differ and this affects the sounds we hear.

FREQUENCY is measured in cycles per second or *hertz* (Hz). A cycle is a complete vibration – the movement of the end of the ruler from one side to the other and back again, for example. One cycle per second is 1 Hz, 50 cycles per second is 50 Hz and so on. Sounds with a high pitch have a greater frequency than low sounds. The human ear can generally detect sounds in the range of 20-20,000 Hz or 20-20,000 vibrations per second. The ability to hear the higher-pitched sounds declines as you get older. Many animals – dogs and bats for example – are capable of hearing sounds of high pitch inaudible to human beings.

AMPLITUDE If you twang your ruler harder it sounds louder. The ruler still vibrates at the same frequency as this is controlled by the length of the exposed end of the ruler, but it is displaced further. The air is also displaced more and travels further before being pulled back again. This distance is called the *amplitude* of the vibration and registers in the ear as a louder noise because the air transmits more energy.

The speed of sound

Sound moves through the air at about 340 metres per second – much, much slower than the speed of light. This is why you see a lightning flash seconds before you hear the crash of thunder. Sound travels slowest in gases, faster in liquids, and fastest in solids. It whizzes through wood at about 4 kilometres per second!

Echoes

Sound travels in straight lines and is reflected back from surfaces it strikes. It is heard as an *echo*. The length of time it takes to receive the echo indicates how far away the object is, and the direction the sound returns along gives you its position. Bats use a system of *echo-location* to gain an image of their environment. They make high-pitched noises as they fly through the air and are constantly listening for the echoes. This is why many species of bats have large ears.

Resonance

If you push a swing there is a certain frequency of pushing at which the swing quickly picks up energy and climbs higher and higher. This is the *natural frequency* of the swing. Different objects have different natural frequencies at which they 'prefer' to vibrate and if you supply them with energy at this frequency they steadily increase the amplitude of their vibrations. This effect is called *resonance*.

Wine glasses have a natural frequency at which they vibrate

The bat's amazing echo-location system.

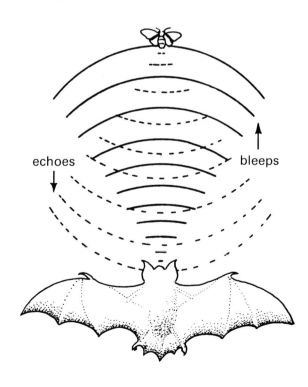

echoes   bleeps

The Tacoma Narrow Bridge in America was set swinging by strong gusting winds in 1940. The alternating eddies of wind tied in with the natural frequency of the bridge and it began swinging more and more wildly until it finally fell apart.

Make Your Own Milk Bottle Orchestra

Fill eight milk bottles with varying depths of water and blow over the tops. Vibrations are set up in the air inside the bottles. The more air there is, the lower the note produced. By carefully adjusting the depths of water you should be able to produce a scale. Now, what are you going to play? Handel's Water Music?

and they will shatter if they are made to vibrate too much. This can happen if someone sings a note at the correct frequency for too long. Even structures like bridges are prone to resonance and have to be carefully designed so they won't damage themselves by wobbling too much.

Resonance can also be produced in a still column of air — which is how the sound is generated in a wind instrument like the sax or flute.

Light Reading

Poor old Blister – he's in the dark about most things, and relies on us to enlighten him! Did you know that perfect darkness, the complete absence of light, is really quite rare? Although it gets harder to see at night, even in your bedroom with the curtains drawn there is still usually a faint glimmer of light visible and you can make out hazy shapes if you look carefully.

We can see objects because they reflect light which enters our eyes through the pupil, a hole of variable size. Inside our eye, the light strikes nerve cells which send messages to the brain that are interpreted as an image. The eye is easily fooled though. Which of these straight lines is the longest?

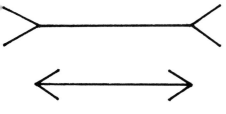

Now try measuring them with a ruler. Are you surprised to find that they are the same length?

Most of the light we see comes from the sun – either directly as sunlight, or indirectly as light generated by the burning of fossil fuels. Our sun is not a particularly large or bright star but it is very near – only 150 million kilometres away – which is why it is such a dominant feature in the sky.

What is light?

Like sound, light can carry energy and it travels in waves, but, unlike sound, it is capable of passing through a vacuum: the light from the sun reaches us across lots of empty space. Light waves are part of the **electromagnetic spectrum**. This is a whole family of waves including infra-red and ultra-violet radiation, X-rays and radio-waves, among others. But more about that in the next chapter.

So, light is thought of as a travelling wave of energy. In the diagram of a lightwave below the distance A to B is called the **wave-length**; the number of times the light describes the shape between A and B in one second is called the **frequency**. The longer the wave-length, the lower the frequency. The eye sees light of different wavelengths as different colours. Red light has the longest wave-

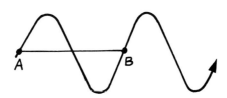

length and violet light the shortest. They are both very small, however – several millionths of a centimetre, or thereabouts.

If you hold an object, such as a ball, up in front of a small bright light it casts a shadow of the same shape as the object on a nearby wall or screen. This occurs because light travels in straight lines. The ball has blocked the light's path and the shadow marks the area the light cannot reach.

Light travels at great speed. The speed of light in a vacuum is believed to be the fastest anything can ever travel in the universe – 300 million metres per second. Even at this speed it still takes over 8 minutes for light from the sun to reach us.

What Is A Light-Year?

A light-year is not a measure of time but of distance. It is how far light would travel in space in a year – that is over 9 million, million kilometres. The nearest star to Earth is over 4½ light-years away, and the nearest galaxy about 2 million light-years! Even if you could travel at the speed of light it would take a long time to get anywhere, but to date the fastest rocket has only reached about a millionth of that speed.

When light hits the surface of a material it is either **reflected** and bounces off, **absorbed** – giving its energy to the molecules or atoms of the surface – or **transmitted** through the material. Materials that allow light to pass through them are said to be **transparent**. When light enters a transparent material such as a glass of water it slows down and is bent or **refracted** as it changes speed. You can see this if you dip the end of a pencil into a glass of water – the pencil appears to bend. The light from the end of the pencil bends as it passes out of the water to travel to your eye, making the pencil seem to bend. This same effect makes the deep floor of a swimming pool look closer to the surface than it actually is. Don't get out of your depth!

Make A Coin Disappear Using Refraction

Place a coin underneath an empty glass. You should be able to see it clearly through the sides. Now fill the glass with water. The coin disappears! Refraction bends light from the coin away from your eye and you can't see it.

If you wear spectacles, the lenses in them use refraction to bend the light entering your eyes to correct any defects in your vision. The lenses either bring rays of light closer together (**convex**) or bend them apart (**concave**).

Colour

Sunlight or the light we see when we switch on a torch seems to be white in colour but it is in fact a mixture of lights of different colours. This was first shown by Sir Isaac Newton in 1666. He shone sunlight through a special-

In normal-sighted people, light entering the eye is focussed onto the retina at the back of the eye-ball. Short- and long-sighted people have to wear spectacles or contact lenses to correct the fault in their vision.

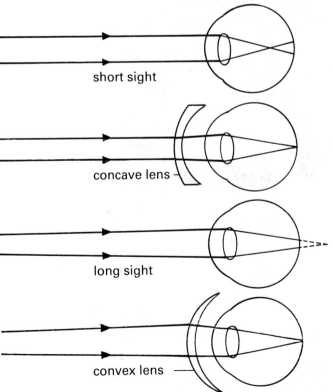

short sight

concave lens

long sight

convex lens

shaped lens called a *prism* which refracted the light so that it spread out into its component colours: red, orange, yellow, green, blue, indigo and violet. This is called the *spectrum* of visible light. The different colours of light separate because they are bent to different degrees depending on their wavelengths. Mixing them together gives a white light again. Objects appear different colours to the eye because they absorb some wavelengths of light and reflect others. If they reflect red light they look red, and so on. If they reflect all the colours they look white and if they absorb all the colours they look black.

If sunlight is shone through a triangular glass block called a prism, it will be split into its component colours – the spectrum of visible light.

See For Yourself!

Paint or crayon the seven colours of the spectrum – red, orange, yellow, green, blue, indigo and violet – onto a spinner made from a piece of white card and a pencil. When you spin the card the colours combine to give a dirty white. It is not pure white because the colours on the spinner are never quite accurate.

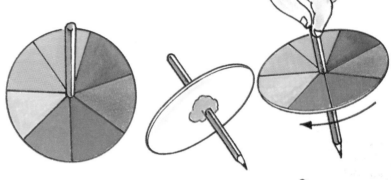

Spectrum is Go!

Hello fellow scholars. Rat here, with the task of filling you in on the rest of the *electromagnetic spectrum.* Well, I don't mind a bit of 'light' work now and again. (Get it?) Sitting in a room during the day, you are surrounded by energy – only some of which you can appreciate. You can see certain wavelengths of light and you will probably feel heat and movements of the air if there is a draught, but that isn't the sum of it.

The room is penetrated by waves of energy that you're just not aware of – electromagnetic waves. All forms of electromagnetic radiation travel at the speed of light – 300,000,000 metres per second, but their wavelengths differ greatly, as you can see on the diagram of the full electromagnetic spectrum.

Radio waves

If there's a radio in the room you can turn it on and listen to some music (sound energy) but where does the sound originate from? It comes from outside the room. The radio is turned to detect invisible energy in the form of *radio waves.*

Radio waves have the longest wavelengths of all electromagnetic waves. They are generated by electrical curents moving backwards and forwards in special circuits. These are then beamed out or transmitted from tall aerial masts. The waves can travel many thousand kilometres around the globe before they are picked up or *received* by your radio set.

The range of wavelengths used in radio communications varies from several thousand metres

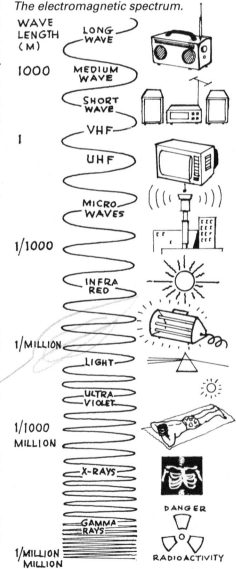

The electromagnetic spectrum.

('long' wave) to several metres (VHF – very high frequency). In between are the 'medium' and 'short' wave wavebands that you find on many portable radios. 'Tuning' changes the frequency of radiation to which the radio is sensitive.

The amount of energy transferred by radio waves is really quite small and needs to be *amplified* to produce a clear sound – which is why radios are run on batteries.

Besides music broadcasts and messages for police, ambulance and taxi services, radio waves are also used to transmit TV pictures and in the operation of *radar*. Radar is an acronym for 'RAdio Detecting And Ranging'. It was developed during the 1930s and is essentially the same as the system of echo-location my cousins the bats have been using for thousands of years. Pulses of short wave radiation are sent out, strike objects and are reflected back. By measuring the time they take to return and their direction, it is then possible to calculate the object's position. Radar was useful in locating night-flying aircraft in the Second World War and nowadays is an essential navigational aid for shipping, particularly in busy sea-lanes like the English Channel.

Microwaves

Microwaves are radio waves of very short wavelength. They are particularly useful for cooking food quickly. In a microwave oven, the energy is absorbed by water molecules in food and these vibrate faster and faster making the food hot. This is a very efficient method of cooking because no energy gets wasted on heating pans or dishes or is 'lost' to the air.

Microwave beams, via satellites, are also used to carry communication links around the world.

Infra-red rays

All hot objects give off infra-red light and there is a large component of infra-red radiation in sunlight which is why it feels warm on our skin. Infra-red lamps are used medically to 'heat-treat' bruised or painful muscles.

Ultra-violet light

Ultra-violet light, known as UV, for short, is also present in sunlight and causes the tanning of pale skins. UV is very powerful and potentially very dangerous. Over-exposure to UV will cause burning and may even lead to more serious skin conditions. This is why you should *always* use tanning lotion if you sunbathe. This screens out most of the harmful UV radiation allowing only less dangerous wavelengths through.

UV is not all bad, however. Because tanning, the action of UV

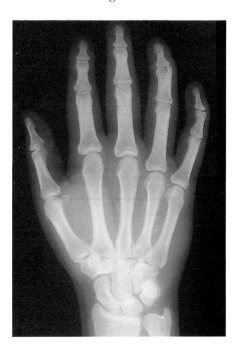

X-rays have very short wavelengths. They can penetrate body tissue easily and are used to take photographs of the human body.

on the skin also causes the formation of vitamin D – a factor vital for healthy bones. Some people need to take vitamin D tablets in winter because they don't receive enough sunlight on their skin.

The *ozone layer* round the Earth is vitally important because it screens out most of the harmful UV radiation we receive from the sun. In recent years the ozone layer has been shrinking fast – partly due to the action of propellant gases used in aerosols. There is already a hole in the ozone layer over the South Pole. You can help reduce damage to the ozone layer by using roll-on or liquid products rather than aerosols. Don't be a squirt if you can help it!

Wilhelm Röntgen discovered X-rays.

X-rays and beyond

X-rays are another form of radiation you'll be very familiar with if you've ever been to the dentist or broken a bone. they were discovered in 1895 by a German scientist, Wilhelm Röntgen, who hadn't the faintest idea what they were, so he called them X-rays – and the name stuck! They are produced by firing a stream of electrons at very high speed at a lead target which absorbs all the energy and then gives off X-rays. X-rays have a very short wavelength and lots of energy and will penetrate substances that are opaque to ordinary light, like wood and thin metals. They fog photographic film and are used to take internal pictures of the human body. The rays pass more easily through flesh than they do denser bone tissue and any cracks or splits in the bones show up.

Softer parts of the body can be seen by feeding the patient a 'barium meal'. (Barium is a metal.) The barium stops the X-ray passing through so that the outline of the internal organ can be seen on photographs.

Because X-rays are so powerful, exposure to them has to be strictly limited and hospitals are very careful in their use nowadays. You may have noticed that your dentist stands behind a screen when he or she takes an X-ray of your mouth. This is because the dentist uses the X-ray machine many times a year and is avoiding over-exposure. X-rays can affect cells in the body but are harmless when correctly used and can even help cure some diseases in a treatment known as *radio-therapy.*

A far more dangerous type of radiation is found beyond X-rays in the electromagnetic spectrum: *gamma rays.* These are waves of a very high frequency and they have great penetrating power. Gamma rays will travel through several centimetres of lead before stopping and are potentially very dangerous. They are produced in nuclear reactions.

Current Affairs

The Minister received an unexpected electric shock the other day – the quarterly electricity bill for the laboratory came through and was bigger than he'd imagined! Nobody likes paying bills but the sheer convenience of having a supply of electricity available in our homes and at work makes our lives a lot easier. We just push in a plug, flick a switch, and there it is.

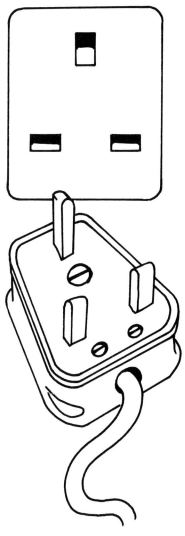

Electricity can be generated in a variety of ways. It is such a useful carrier of energy because it's so easy to channel between points and it can do so many useful things. Pylons can carry electricity from one side of a continent to another and even in areas remote from grid supplies people can make their own electricity using generators or they can run appliances from batteries. Electricity is great stuff, but what exactly is it?

Well, the ancient Greeks wondered much the same thing, particularly a chap called Thales (640-546 BC). Early investigations into the nature of electricity were all concerned with *static electricity* – the stationary charge that builds up on or within an object.

Static electricity

Thales found that when he rubbed a lump of amber (fossilised resin) with a hank of wool, the amber was left with the ability to pick up bits of feather and straw. The nature of the force generated by rubbing the amber remained a mystery for many hundred of years but is now quite easy to explain with our knowledge of atomic structure.

Atoms are made up of a nucleus containing protons and neutrons. This nucleus is orbited by electrons. Electric charge is carried by the electrons and protons in every atom. The electrons have a negative (−) charge and the protons have a positive (+) charge. The neutrons have no charge. The electrons are held in orbit around the nucleus by a force of *electrostatic attraction*: that is opposite charges attract one another and like ('similar') charges repel each other. Because the number of electrons in an atom is normally the same as the number of protons, atoms have no overall charge and are said to be 'neutral'.

Large atoms have lots of electrons whizzing round their nuclei and the outer ones are so far away that they are only weakly held by attraction to the protons. They can easily be displaced from their orbits. If a material gains or loses electrons, there will no longer be a balance between the + and − charges within it and the material becomes charged.

When Thales rubbed his amber with the wool, electrons were stroked off atoms at the surface of the amber and were passed to the atoms of the wool. The amber was left with an overall positive charge (+) and the wool gained an overall negative charge (−).

The amber then picked up bits of fluff because its positive-charge attracted the negatively-charged electrons contained in the atoms of the fluff.

This idea of static electricity took several thousands of years to understand properly. Still, Thales didn't go without reward: the negatively-charged particles in atoms were called 'electrons' in recognition of his early work. (**Elektron** is the Greek word for amber!)

You generate static electric charges when you comb your hair or pull a woollen jumper off from over a shirt or blouse containing synthetic fibres. Again, electrons are stripped away from atoms of one material and passed to those of another. If the difference in electrical charge that builds up between the two surfaces is great enough, you can get sparks bridging the gap. The crackling noise that you may sometimes hear when you comb your hair or undress is the sound made by lots of these small electrical *discharges*.

Sparks occur because, where possible, electrical energy will always move from an area of high voltage to one of a lower voltage. The difference between the high voltage and the lower voltage is called the *potential difference*. Potential difference is measured in *volts* (V) after Count Alessandro Volta (1745-1827), an Italian nobleman renowned for his early work on electricity.

What is lightning?
The British scientist William Wall suspected as early as 1708 that lightning flashes were caused by discharges of static electricity between the clouds and the ground, but the American Benjamin Franklin (1706 – 1790) was the first to actually show it.

Lightning occurs because in certain conditions large negative charges build up at the bottom of rain-clouds. This means there is a great potential difference between the clouds and the ground. Air normally acts as an insulator but its insulating capacity breaks down in such a high potential difference and electricity flows down to the Earth following the easiest and shortest path. This is why tall buildings and trees tend to get hit. The 'flash' is light produced by excited air molecules and the thunderclap

Benjamin Franklin's 1752 experiment with a kite in a storm. He showed that lightning was caused by static electricity, but he was very lucky not to lose his life by doing so. The amount of energy transferred by a lightning flash can be massive – up to 300 million joules.

is the noise created by this giant spark.

In 1752, Franklin flew a kite on a long wire into the bottom of some thunderclouds. The wire was attached to a silk thread which he held in his hands, with a metal key suspended from it. Charge from the cloud travelled down the wire and collected in the key so that when Franklin brought his finger close to the key a spark jumped from it to his finger and the charge ran through his body and into the ground. He showed that lightning was indeed due to static electricity but he was very lucky not to be killed. The amount of energy tranferred by a lightning flash can be massive (up to 300 million joules) and the very next person to try Franklin's experiment was frazzled. Franklin survived to invent the **lightning conductor** – a sharp metal spike placed at the top of buildings and connected to a continuous metal strip that runs down into the

FLY 1 *Have you heard the saying 'Lightning never strikes twice in the same place'?*

FLY 2 *How wrong can you be: one man was hit seven times. Now that's what I call unlucky!*

41

ground below. It safely conveys lightning to the earth, leaving buildings unharmed.

Conductors and insulators

Some materials are better at conveying electrical charges than others and are said to be good *conductors*. Metals are excellent conductors. If a material doesn't conduct electricity it is called an *insulator*. Plastics, rubber, ceramics and glass are all good examples of good insulators.

These properties are again due to the way electrons are held around atoms. In conductors, the outer electrons are so loosely held to the atom that they pass randomly between atoms forming a sort of charged electron cloud. If you apply a potential difference across a metal this cloud drifts towards the positive potential and this movement of electrons constitutes an *electric current*. The greater the potential difference the faster the electrons move giving a greater current. Current is measured in *amperes* (A) or 'amps' for short, named after the French scientist Ampère (1775-1836).

Electric current and the battery

Scientists had no means of generating steady electrical currents until the invention of the first batteries at the end of the eighteenth century. The Italian scientists Luigi Galvani (1737-1798) and Volta both found that a current could be produced by bringing together two different metals in moist, acidic conditions. (The strange feeling you get when you accidentally touch a piece of foil against a dental filling is due to the production of a small electrical current. There is a difference in potential between the mercury used in your fillings and the aluminium of the foil – and horrible it is too!) Volta built giant structures, known as Voltaic piles, made of alternating discs of two different metals and wadding soaked in acid, in an attempt to produce greater currents.

Today, batteries are a little more sophisticated in their construction, but work on essentially the same scientific principle. Torch batteries are what are known as 'dry cells': Volta's soaked discs have been replaced by two reacting chemicals. However, car batteries still rely on a wet acidic solution. They are very large and heavy and must be kept upright.

The need for development of a small but powerful and efficient battery is the one major factor holding back the wide-scale use of electric vehicles. They are a great idea as they wouldn't need to run off our dwindling resources of fossil fuel and consequently wouldn't produce any harmful exhaust gases.

FLY 1 *What did Blister do when the Prof's battery went missing?*

FLY 2 *Nothing – it wasn't his 'volt'!*

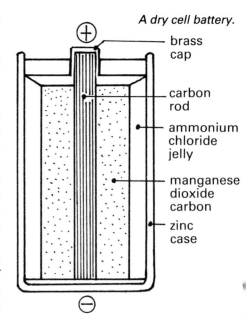

A dry cell battery.

- brass cap
- carbon rod
- ammonium chloride jelly
- manganese dioxide carbon
- zinc case

Poles Apart

I often stop to wonder what it is that makes me so incredibly attractive. Is it my good looks, my charm – or is it my great natural modesty?! I have what you might call a 'magnetic personality' and real magnets – the sort you can pick up bits of metal with – are almost (but not quite) as interesting.

Anything that attracts iron is called a **magnet** and the force involved is known as **magnetism**. People have been wondering about it for quite some time. The ancient Greeks and the Chinese both made observations on the nature of magnetism over 2000 years ago. They noticed that a form of iron ore called **magnetite** that they quarried from the ground was weakly attractive to iron. The Greeks thought that bits of metal stuck to it because it had lots of tiny hooks on its surface, but they were wrong!

Smart sailors in the Middle Ages used another property of magnetite to help them navigate the seas. They found that freely suspended rods of the ore always swung to point in the same direction, almost exactly corresponding to a line running north-south. In effect they had invented the **compass**. They placed the swinging ore at the bow of the ship where it became known as **lodestone** or 'leading stone'.

Today you can buy magnets in all shapes and sizes from the long and rectangular bar-magnet to the horseshoe-shaped magnet. Magnets will only attract certain materials – the metals **iron**, **nickel** and **cobalt**, and alloys made from them. These substances are said to be **ferromagnetic**. Bar-magnets are sometimes made from steel which is a mixture of iron with carbon but most are alloys such as Alnico (ALuminium, NIckel and CObalt). They pick up things like steel paper-clips and iron nails, but not aluminium foil or paper or glass – these materials are **non-magnetic**.

Magnetic poles

You can demonstrate most of the properties of magnets for yourself using simple bar-magnets and iron-filings that you can buy from a toyshop or hardware store.

Dip a bar-magnet into the iron-filings. Notice how the filings stick all over the magnet but cluster most strongly around the opposite ends of the bar. These are known as the **poles** of the magnet, where the forces of magnetic attraction are the strongest.

North Poles and South Poles

Suspend the bar horizontally at its centre with a length of string so that it can rotate freely. The magnet will always end up set in a direction roughly north-south. The end of the magnet pointing north is said to be the **North-seeking pole** – abbreviated to **North Pole** or **N**. The end of the magnet pointing south is the **South-seeking**

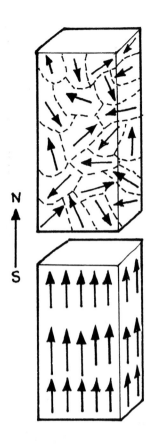

Top *Unmagnetised iron.*
Above *Magnetised iron.*

The lines of force made when the ends of two magnets are put together. Point X is called a neutral point – where two like poles face each other the field of one magnet cancels out the field of the other and so there are no lines of force.

pole – abbreviated to **South Pole** or **S**. You will often find that the ends of a magnet are stamped with the letters N and S to distinguish them, or sometimes the north pole is painted red.

FORCES BETWEEN POLES Take two bar-magnets. Bring the north pole of one magnet close to the south pole of another (or vice versa). You will feel a strong force of attraction between them and they will stick together. Sometimes this force can be so great that you can't pull them apart and you will have to slide them over each other to separate them.

Now, turn one of the magnets round and bring either a south pole up to a south pole or a north pole up to another north pole. You can't do it. Sometimes, you can't even push them together – there is such a strong force of *repulsion* between them.

These facts can be summed up in a simple law: *Like Poles Repel, Unlike Poles Attract.*

The magnetic field

The region around a magnet in which it will exert a force on a ferromagnetic object is called a *magnetic field*. It gets weaker the further away you get from the magnet. You can get the idea of the shape of the magnetic field around a bar-magnet by placing two magnets on a sheet of card

and sprinkling iron-filings evenly around them. If you gently tap the card, the filings form up into curved lines that run between the north and south poles.

The British scientist Michael Faraday (1791–1867) said that these curved lines represented invisible *lines of force* that run from the north to south poles of magnets. (These actually exist in three dimensions but you can only show two on the flat card.) Magnets repel and attract because their individual lines of force interact. But how is a magnet produced?

Making a magnet

In a magnetic material, such as iron, each atom behaves as a tiny magnet each with a north pole and south pole. In a piece of un-magnetised iron these tiny magnets are all arranged higgledy-piggledy and their effects cancel each other out. However, in magnetised iron, these tiny magnets are all arranged in the same direction and their effects add up to give a strong magnetic field. Because of this arrangement you can break the magnet at any point along its length to produce more magnets each with a north and south pole. This polarity results from the way the electrons spin round the nuclei. In a strong magnet they all spin the same way. For such small things electrons are jolly important!

The magnetic field around a magnet will *magnetise* a piece of iron placed into it. This is called *magnetic induction* and you can see it happen when you dip a bar-magnet into a box of pins. A string of pins can be picked up, each acting as if it had a north-south pole. The pins retain some of their polarity when you take them out

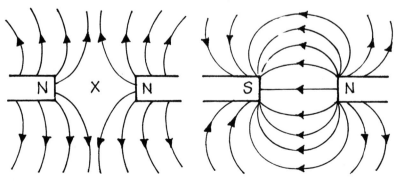

of the field – which can be very annoying to a dressmaker. Pick up one pin and you get half a box!

Magnets can also be made by stroking a length of iron repeatedly in one direction only with the same pole of a magnet. By this action the tiny magnets inside are lined up and the iron is magnetised. Alternatively, you can destroy the powers of a magnet simply by heating it to a high temperature. The tiny magnets inside become all mixed up once more and the material is de-magnetised.

The Earth's magnetic field

The Earth itself acts as a giant magnet with lines of force running from one pole down in the Antarctic (the South Pole) to another in northern Canada: the *Magnetic North Pole*. This is about 1600km distant from the true, geographical North Pole. The Earth's magnetic north pole attracts the north pole of a suspended bar or a compass, which means it must really be the *south* pole of a magnet. No one is quite sure why the Earth acts as a giant magnet. However, its magnetic field is strong enough to induce magnetism in iron or steel structures on its surface. In the northern hemisphere, iron railings have a south pole induced at the top and a north pole at the bottom. You can test this yourself using a pocket compass. The polarities are reversed in the southern hemisphere.

Electromagnetism

The major breakthrough in the study of magnetism was made in 1820 when a Dane called Hans Oersted noticed that a magnetic field was produced when an electric current flowed through a wire.

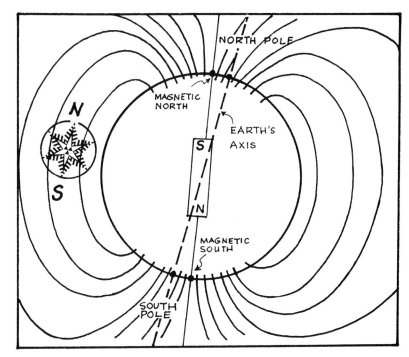

This effect is known as *electromagnetism*. A really strong magnet can be made by simply wrapping lots of turns of wire around a central iron core and passing a current through them. Electromagnets made from soft magnetic materials such as iron are very useful because they cease to be attractive if there is no current flowing. Scrapyards employ large electromagnets that will pick up old cars and then drop them when the power is turned off.

A little after Oersted's observations, Faraday then showed that an electric current could be generated by moving a magnet inside a coil and this method – called *electromagnetic induction* – is the basis for most of our electricity production.

Since those early days of investigation, the existence of magnets and electromagnetism has made possible many different things – from electric motors to telephones to tape recorders. Our lives would be very strange without them.

The Earth's magnetic field: it is almost as if there were a giant bar-magnet buried in the Earth's core. The Earth's magnetic S-pole lies under the geographical N-pole.

FLY 1 *I think Blister must be magnetic*

FLY 2 *Yes – he always seems to attract trouble!*

Glossary

Ampere A unit used to measure electric current. It describes the speed at which a fixed number of electrons flow along a wire. The faster they travel the greater the current.

Atom The smallest particle of an element that can take part in a chemical reaction. It is composed of an equal number of protons and electrons and a variable number of neutrons.

Capillarity The movement of liquids in fine tubes. It is caused by the different degrees of attraction between the molecules of the liquid for each other and for the molecules of the tube.

Compound A substance made up of two or more different types of atoms. The atoms are chemically combined in fixed proportions, water for example always contains 2 hydrogen atoms for every 1 oxygen atom.

Conduction The flow of thermal energy or electricity through a substance. Metals are good **conductors** of both heat and electricity. Substances that do not conduct well are called **insulators.**

Convection The movement of thermal energy through a liquid or gas due to movement of the hot substance.

Density The mass per unit volume of a substance – measured in kg/m^3. It describes how much matter is present in a given space.

Electricity A term used to describe phenomena caused by electric charge. Charge is due to the presence or absence of electrons. Electricity can flow, in the form of a **current,** or be stationary – **static electricity.**

Electromagnetic spectrum The spread of radiation of different frequencies that includes radiowaves, infra-red, visible light, ultra-violet, X-rays and gamma rays.

Electron The negatively-charged (−) particle found around the nucleus of an atom. Small and light, the flow of electrons constitutes an electric current.

Electrostatic attraction The force of attraction between two particles or objects of opposite electrical charge: + and −. It is this force that keeps electrons in orbit around the nucleus of an atom.

Element A substance made up entirely of atoms of the same type. The atoms each contain the same number of protons in their nuclei.

Force The outside push that tends to change the motion of an object. It can start it moving, speed it up, or slow it down.

Friction The resistance you can feel when you try to slide two surfaces over each other. It is due to attractions between their molecules.

Gravity The force of attraction between masses due to the mass of the objects. The Earth's gravitational attraction causes objects to fall to its surface.

Isotopes Different atoms of an element that have the same number of protons but different numbers of neutrons. Thus they differ in mass.

Magnetism The force of attraction produced by a magnet for objects made of ferromagnetic substances.

Mass A measure of the 'enertia' of an object. The greater an object's mass, the harder it is to get it moving by pushing it.

Matter A general term for *all* substances in the universe. Matter has mass and takes up space.

Molecule The smallest portion of a substance that can exist on its own and still have all the properties of the original substance.

Neutron The uncharged particle in an atom's nucleus. Their number can vary, giving rise to isotopes.

Nuclear energy The energy released by changes in atoms. During the changes a tiny amount of mass is lost which is converted into a gigantic amount of energy.

Nuclear fusion The process that fuels the sun. It involves simple atoms coming together to form larger atoms. A lot of energy is released in the form of radiation.

Ozone layer A special layer in the atmosphere that protects the Earth from excessive harmful ultra-violet light. Ozone is a form of oxygen.

Proton The positively-charged fundamental particle in an atom's nucleus. The number of protons – the atomic number – decides what element an atom belongs to.

State The form in which matter exists: either solid, liquid or gas. It depends on the arrangement of a substance's molecules.

Solvent, solute A solvent is a liquid in which other substances – solutes – will dissolve. Together they form a solution.

Surface tension The mutual attraction between identical molecules (cohesion) in a liquid that seems to produce a 'skin' at the surface.

Visible spectrum The span of different colours of light as seen in a rainbow. They combine to give white light and can be produced by passing white light through a special lens called a prism.

Voltage A measure of the difference in electrical potential energy between two points. The greater the difference the faster electricity will flow between the two points.

ZZZZZZZ! The Professor asleep again!

46